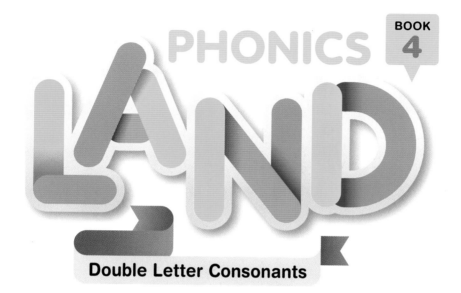

PHONICS

BOOK 4

LAND

Double Letter Consonants

YBM

Contents

Letters and Sounds
Combinations of letters and the target sounds are introduced.

Words
Students learn to recognize the words that have the beginning or ending sounds of the target letters.

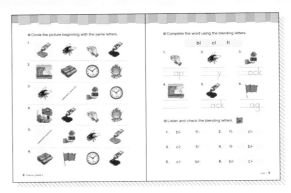

Practice
Students practice choosing the correct picture for the given pictures, letters or words.

Write and Check
Students practice writing and checking the correct blending letters for the target words.

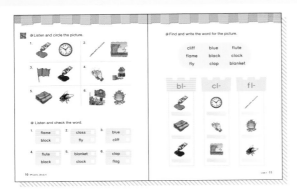

Listen and Check
Students further practice identifying the sounds and the words by reading and listening.

Write
Students review the blending letters and words of the unit.

Let's Read
Students practice the target sounds and words by reading simple sentences.

Choose and Write
Students practice reading the sentence and choosing the correct word.

Review & Challenge

The Review provides practice of the materials from the previous four units by using a variety of exercises focusing on the target sounds of letters and words.

The Challenge offers sessions to review the entire book. It reinforces students' phonics skills with various exercises and a test.

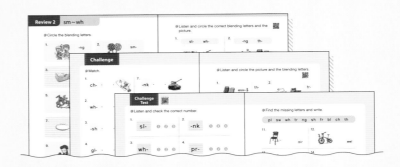

Special Features

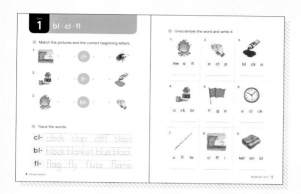

⟡ Workbook ⟡

Students review what they learned in class.
This can be used as homework or further practice.

⟡ How to use QR codes ⟡

Scan QR codes on the content pages, then you can use all of the listening sounds and flash animations, such as chants, stories, and listening questions.

e-learning Scan e-learning QR codes, then you can use e-learning for self-study.

game Scan game QR codes, then you can enjoy the phonics games.

• Note for Teachers •

The ultimate goal of the book is to help students be able to read and write words even if they encounter a new word. Therefore, students should be encouraged to listen and to identify the sounds of the letters, not to memorize the spellings of the words.

bl · cl · fl

 ● Listen and repeat.

b l → bl

bl + anket → blanket

c l → cl

cl + ock → clock

f l → fl

fl + ag → flag

🔊 Listen and repeat.

bl

blanket   blue   black   block

cl

clock   class   clap   cliff

fl

flag   fly   flute   flame

Chant Along!

● Circle the picture beginning with the same letters.

1.

2.

3.

4.

5.

6.

● Complete the word using the blending letters.

bl   cl   fl

1.

_____ ap

2.

_____ y

3.

_____ ock

4.

_____ iff

5.

_____ ack

6.

_____ ag

● Listen and check the blending letters.

1.   bl-   fl-   2.   fl-   cl-

3.   cl-   fl-   4.   fl-   bl-

5.   cl-   bl-   6.   bl-   cl-

● Listen and circle the picture.

1.

2.

3.

4.

5.

6.

● Listen and check the word.

1.
flame ☐
block ☐

2.
class ☐
fly ☐

3.
blue ☐
cliff ☐

4.
flute ☐
black ☐

5.
blanket ☐
clock ☐

6.
clap ☐
flag ☐

● Find and write the word for the picture.

cliff   blue   flute

flame   black   clock

fly   clap   blanket

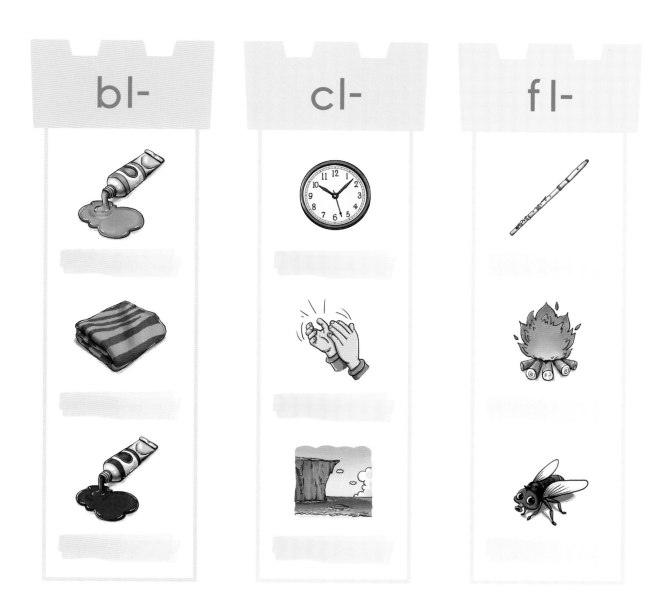

bl-   cl-   f l-

Look at the clock.

It is ten in the morning.

It is time for art class!

I paint my cup blue and black.

Wow, it looks pretty!

My friends clap for me.

● Choose the correct word and write.

1. Children look at the blue _____.

   flag   fly

2. It is time for English _____.

   clock   class

3. The girl paints a cup green and _____.

   block   black

4. Mom and dad _____ for the boy.

   clap   cliff

5. The _____ looks warm.

   block   blanket

 ⦿ Listen and repeat.

b   r   →   br

br + ead → bread

c   r   →   cr

cr + ow → crow

f   r   →   fr

fr + iend → friend

🔊 Listen and repeat.

br

b**r**ead   b**r**ide   b**r**idge   b**r**ush

cr

c**r**ow   c**r**ab   c**r**ane   c**r**y

fr

f**r**iend   f**r**ame   f**r**uit   f**r**ost

Chant Along!

⬤ Circle the picture beginning with the same letters.

1.

2.

3.

4.

5.

6.

● Complete the word using the blending letters.

br   cr   fr

1.

____uit

2.

____ab

3.

____ide

4.

____y

5.

____ush

6.

____ost

● Listen and check the blending letters.

1.   fr-   br-   2.   cr-   fr-

3.   cr-   br-   4.   fr-   br-

5.   fr-   cr-   6.   cr-   br-

🔘 Listen and circle the picture.

1.

2.

3.

4.

5.

6.

🔘 Listen and check the word.

1.
cry ☐
friend ☐

2.
crow ☐
brush ☐

3.
frost ☐
bridge ☐

4.
frame ☐
bread ☐

5.
crab ☐
bride ☐

6.
crane ☐
friend ☐

● Find and write the word for the picture.

bread   crane   frost

friend   brush   cry

crab   fruit   bride

cr-       

_____   _____   _____

fr-      

_____   _____   _____

br-      

_____   _____   _____

There was frost at night.

The world is white and cold.

A crow is in the tree.

It is crying loudly.

It looks cold.

A crab is on the bridge.

It is eating some bread.

It looks hungry.

○ Choose the correct word and write.

1.

There is a _____ on the table.

| brush | bread |

2.

A crow is on the _____.

| crane | bridge |

3.

The _____ is in the car.

| bride | friend |

4.

A _____ is walking sideways.

| crane | crab |

5.

The _____s look very tasty.

| fruit | bread |

 🔘 Listen and repeat.

g   l → gl

gl + ass → glass

p   l → pl

pl + ane → plane

s   l → sl

sl + ide → slide

Listen and repeat.

gl

glass   glove   globe   glue

pl

plane   plate   plant   plum

sl

slide   sled   slim   slice

Chant Along!

● Circle the blending letters for the picture.

1.

sl-

pl-

2.

gl-

pl-

3.

sl-

gl-

4.

pl-

sl-

5.

gl-

pl-

6.

pl-

sl-

7.

sl-

pl-

8.

gl-

pl-

● Find the word for each picture and write.

slidetrglasseesledbrplatesleglovegplane

1.

_____

2.

_____

3.

_____

4.

_____

5.

_____

6.

_____

● Listen and check the blending letters.

1. gl-   pl-   2. sl-   gl-

3. sl-   pl-   4. pl-   sl-

5. gl-   sl-   6. pl-   gl-

● Listen and circle the picture.

1.

2.

3.

4.

5.

6.

● Listen and check the word.

1. ☐ slide ☐ plant ☐ glass

2. ☐ plane ☐ sled ☐ glove

3. ☐ globe ☐ slice ☐ plant

4. ☐ plum ☐ glue ☐ slide

● Find the word for each picture and write.

sdragoneprintetrdrivepltrumpetdrepressplrtrack

1.

_____

- - - - - - - - - - - - - -

_____

2.

_____

- - - - - - - - - - - - - -

_____

3.

_____

- - - - - - - - - - - - - -

_____

4.

_____

- - - - - - - - - - - - - -

_____

5.

_____

- - - - - - - - - - - - - -

_____

6.

_____

- - - - - - - - - - - - - -

_____

● Listen and check the blending letters.

1.   dr-   pr-

2.   tr-   pr-

3.   tr-   dr-

4.   pr-   tr-

5.   dr-   tr-

6.   dr-   pr-

⚫ Listen and circle the picture.

1.

2.

3.

4.

5.

6.

⚫ Listen and check the word.

1. ☐ track   ☐ print   ☐ trumpet

2. ☐ drive   ☐ press   ☐ trace

3. ☐ dress   ☐ truck   ☐ prince

4. ☐ trace   ☐ drive   ☐ dragon

● Find and circle. Then write.

dress   trumpet   press

prize   truck   drive

trace   print   dragon

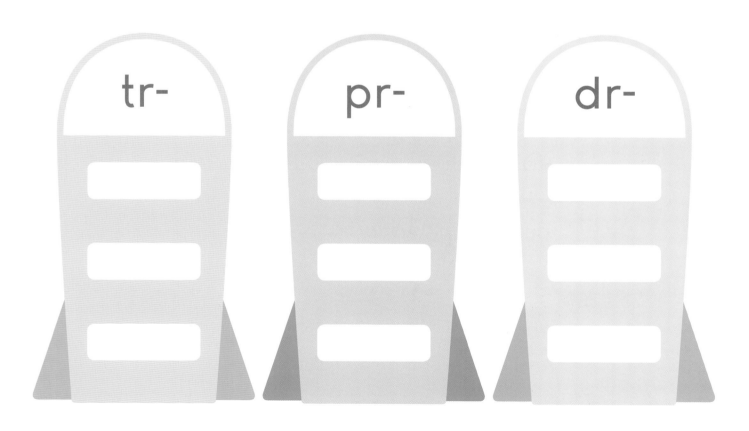

tr-   pr-   dr-

I have two dragon friends.

Their names are Prince and Princess.

This is Prince.

He is strong and handsome.

He likes trucks and trumpets.

This is Princess.

She is pretty and cute.

She likes dresses and drums.

● Choose the correct word and write.

1. The boy has three _____ s .

   truck   trace

2. The _____ is big and shiny.

   trace   prize

3. The _____ is strong and handsome.

   prince   trace

4. The girl likes a _____ and a hat.

   trumpet   dress

5. This is my _____ friend.

   dragon   dress

● Circle the blending letters.

1.

tr-

fr-

br-

2.

sl-

cl-

pl-

3.

pl-

pr-

bl-

4.

fr-

cr-

bl-

5.

bl-

fl-

cl-

6.

cr-

gl-

dr-

7.

br-

cr-

tr-

8.

cr-

tr-

sl-

9.

bl-

pr-

sl-

10.

sl-

gl-

pl-

Listen to the sound and circle the picture.

1.

2.

3.

4.

5.

6.

7.

8.

9.

10.

● Circle the picture beginning with the given letters.

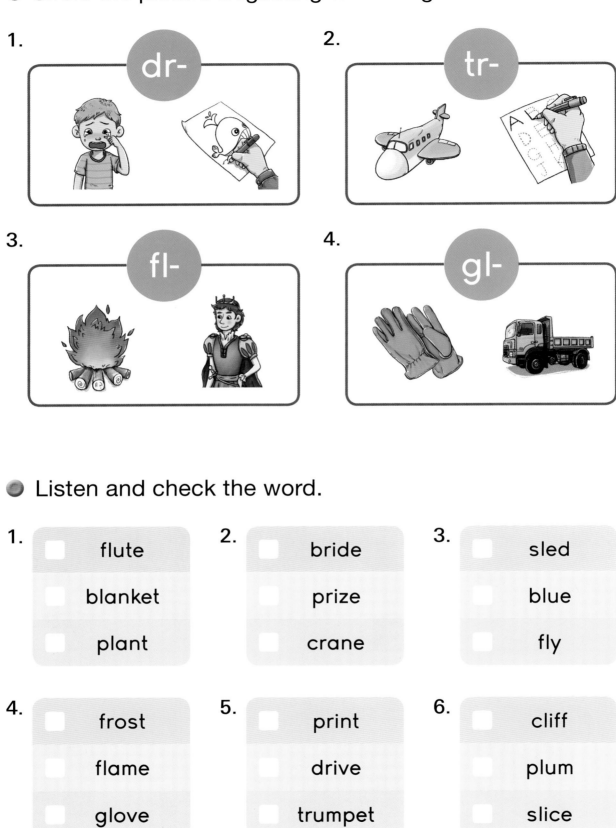

1. dr-

2. tr-

3. fl-

4. gl-

● Listen and check the word.

1.
- ☐ flute
- ☐ blanket
- ☐ plant

2.
- ☐ bride
- ☐ prize
- ☐ crane

3.
- ☐ sled
- ☐ blue
- ☐ fly

4.
- ☐ frost
- ☐ flame
- ☐ glove

5.
- ☐ print
- ☐ drive
- ☐ trumpet

6.
- ☐ cliff
- ☐ plum
- ☐ slice

Unscramble and write the word for the picture.

1.

a g l f

_____

2.

s g a s l

_____

3.

i t r p n

_____

4.

r w a d

_____

5.

r b e i d

_____

6.

a r m e f

_____

7.

n l a p t

_____

8.

l c b k a

_____

9.

w o r c

_____

 ● Listen and repeat.

s   m   →   sm

sm + ile → smile

s   n   →   sn

sn + ail → snail

s   t   →   st

st + amp → stamp

s   w   →   sw

sw + an → swan

● Listen and repeat.

sm

smile

smell

smoke

sn

snail

snack

snore

st

stamp

stop

stone

sw

swan

swim

sweet

Chant Along!

● Read and circle the picture.

1. smile

2. swim

3. stamp

4. smoke

5. snore

6. sweet

● Circle the blending letters and write the word.

1.

sw
st

_____ eet

2.

st
sn

_____ op

3.

sw
sm

_____ ell

4.

sn
sm

_____ ore

5.

sm
sw

_____ an

6.

sn
st

_____ ack

● Listen and check the blending letters.

1.
sm- ☐
st- ☐
sw- ☐

2.
sn- ☐
sw- ☐
st- ☐

3.
st- ☐
sm- ☐
sn- ☐

4.
sm- ☐
sw- ☐
sn- ☐

🌑 Listen and circle the picture.

1.

2.

3.

4.

5.

6.

🌑 Listen and circle the words. Then match.

1.
| stop |
| snail |

2.
| swim |
| smell |

3.
| stone |
| stamp |

4.
| snore |
| smoke |

● Find and write the word for the picture.

snack   stop   smile   stone

sweet   snail   smell   swan

sw-

_____

_____

st-

_____

_____

sn-

_____

_____

sm-

_____

_____

I am a little snail.

I go to the cold and clean lake.

Look, there are flowers.

Mmm... they smell so sweet.

Look, there are stones.

I stop and look at them for a moment.

Finally I am at the lake.

I swim in this lake like a swan.

● Choose the correct word and write.

1.

It is a white _____ .

swim   swan

2.

The snacks _____ so good.

smell   smile

3.

There is a cute _____ on the flower.

snail   sweet

4.

The girl stops and looks at the _____s.

smoke   stone

5.

They _____ in the sea.

swim   swan

Unit 6 ng · nk

  Listen and repeat.

wi + ng → wing

go + ng → gong

wi + nk → wink

ba + nk → bank

● Listen and repeat.

ng

wing

string

sing

swing

gong

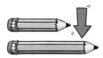

long

nk

wink

sink

pink

drink

bank

tank

Chant Along!

● Read and circle the picture.

1. wing

2. drink

3. sing

4. wink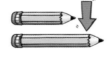

5. pink

6. gong

● Circle the blending letters and write the word.

1.

ng

nk

dri

2.

ng

nk

wi

3.
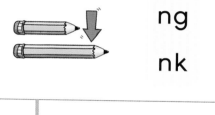
ng

nk

lo

4.

ng

nk

si

5.

ng

nk

wi

6.
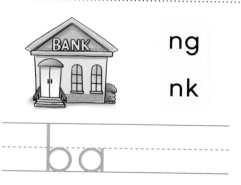
ng

nk

ba

● Listen and check the blending letters.

1.
-ng ☐

-nk ☐

2.
-ng ☐

-nk ☐

3.
-ng ☐

-nk ☐

4.
-ng ☐

-nk ☐

Listen and circle the picture.

1.

2.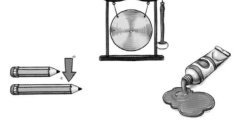

3.

4.

5.

6.

Listen and circle the words. Then match.

1.
| sing |
| gong |

2.
| wink |
| pink |

3.
| drink |
| tank |

4.
| swing |
| wing |

● Find and write the word for the picture.

swing   long   tank

bank   wing

string   drink   wink

Let's Read!

Today is the spring festival.

People have a party in the park.

They sing and dance merrily.

They eat and drink happily.

Look! There is a blue bird with pink wings.

It is a fun festival.

Choose the correct word and write.

1. The girls _____ and dance on the stage.

sing   gong

2. The family eat and _____ in the park.

wink   drink

3. The bird has a _____ around its leg.

wings   string

4. The girl has a _____ flower on her hair.

pink   swing

5. There is a _____ in the kitchen.

sink   swing

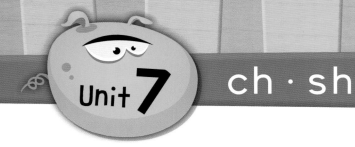

Unit 7 ch · sh

 ◉ Listen and repeat.

ch + air → chair

bea + ch → beach

sh + ip → ship

wa + sh → wash

Listen and repeat.

ch

chair

cheese

chick

beach

branch

bench

sh

ship

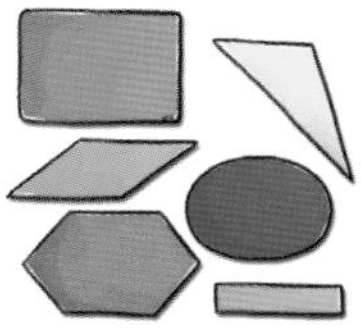

shape

shell

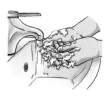

wash

dish

flash

Chant Along!

● Circle the picture beginning or ending with the given letters.

1. **sh-**

2. **-ch**

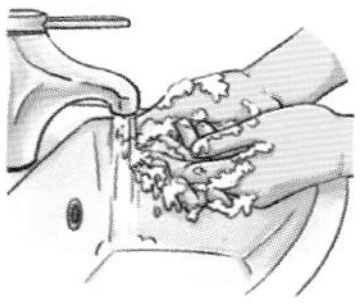

3. **ch-**

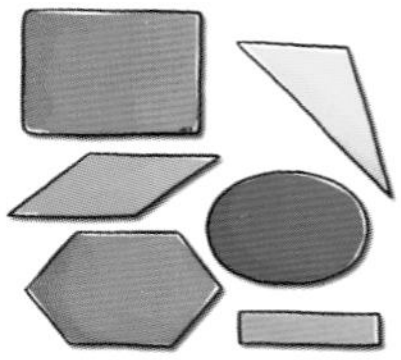

4. **-sh**

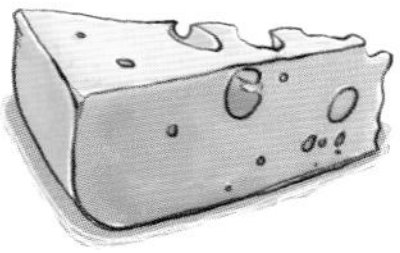

5. **sh-**

6. **-ch**

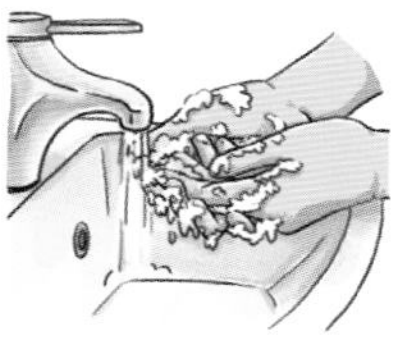

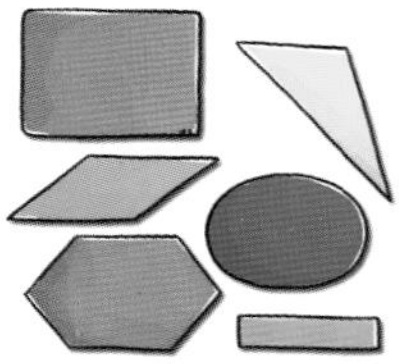

Listen and circle the correct blending letters. Then write the word.

1.
ch   sh

di

2.
sh   ch

bea

3.
sh   ch

ben

4.
sh   ch

ip

5.
ch   sh

eese

6.
sh   ch

wa

7.
ch   sh

ape

8.
ch   sh

ick

🔵 Listen and circle the picture.

1.

2.

3.
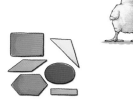

4.

5.

6.

🔵 Check the word.

1.

☐ flash
☐ beach

2.

☐ ship
☐ cheese

3.

☐ wash
☐ flash

4.

☐ shell
☐ chair

● Find and write the word for the picture.

chick   wash   branch   dish

cheese   beach   shell   ship

sh

ch

This is my family's picture.

Dad was running on the beach
with our dog.

Mom was eating cheese
under the beach parasol.

My brother was looking at the shell
with a round shape.

Me?

I took this photo of our family.

Choose the correct word and write.

1.

This is a picture of my pet _____ .

bench   chick

2.

The girl looks at the clock with a round

_____ .

ship   shape

3.

The boy is eating _____ on the table.

cheese   shell

4.

The cook was running with the _____ es.

dish   flash

5.

A dog is eating snacks on the _____ .

branch   bench

e-learning   game

  Listen and repeat.

th + in → thin

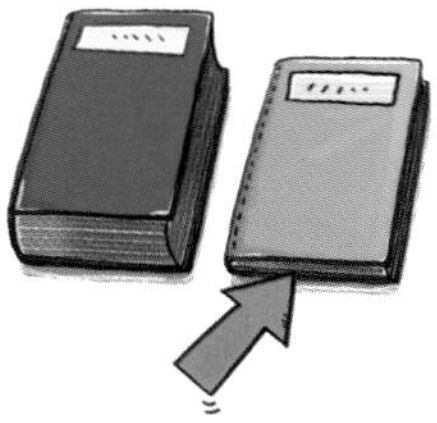

clo + th → cloth

wh + ale → whale

Listen and repeat.

th

thin
- - - - - ->

thick
- - - - - - ->

bath
- - - - - - ->

cloth
- - - - - - - ->

math
- - - - - - - ->

teeth
- - - - - - ->

wh

whale
- - - - - - ->

white
- - - - - ->

wheel
- - - - - - ->

wheat
- - - - - - ->

whip
- - - - - ->

whisper
- - - - - - - ->

Chant Along!

Circle the picture beginning or ending with the given letters.

1. wh-

2. -th

3. -th

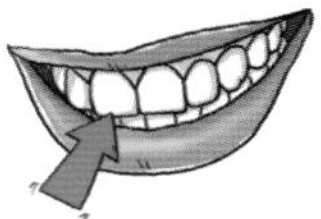

4. wh-

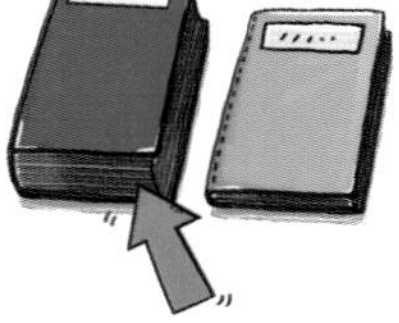

5. wh-

6. -th

Listen and circle the correct blending letters. Then write the word.

1. wh   th

in

2. th   wh

ip

3. th   wh

ite

4. wh   th

ma

5. th   wh

tee

6. wh   th

eel

7. th   wh

ick

8. wh   th

clo

● Listen to the word and circle the picture.

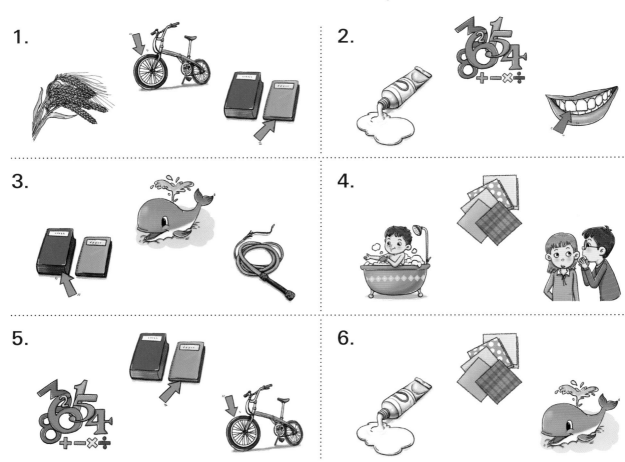

● Check the word.

1. 
- [ ] cloth
- [ ] bath

2. 
- [ ] white
- [ ] whale

3. 
- [ ] whisper
- [ ] wheel

4. 
- [ ] thin
- [ ] teeth

Find and write the word for the picture.

whip   bath   math   wheat

whale   teeth   thick   whisper

th

wh

Mom and I went to an aquarium.

I saw a big white whale.

Its fins were huge and thick.

The whale made a low sound.

It was like a whisper.

I think it is a wonderful animal.

Choose the correct word and write.

1. I saw a big _____ monkey.

white	whip

2. The math book is very _____ .

thick	thin

3. The front _____ is big.

wheat	wheel

4. A _____ makes a low sound.

whale	wheat

5. The _____ is colorful.

teeth	cloth

● Circle the blending letters.

1.
-ng

-nk

2.
sm-

sw-

3.
th-

ch-

4.
wh-

sh-

5.
-th

-ch

6.
sh-

wh-

7.
-ch

-sh

8.
sn-

sh-

9.
sm-

-nk

10.
ch-

th-

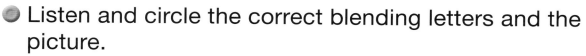 Listen and circle the correct blending letters and the picture.

1.

st-   wh-

2.

-ng   th-

3.

th-   sw-

4.

ch-   sn-

5.

sh-   -th

6.

-nk   -sh

7.

-ch   -ng

8.

sn-   wh-

Circle the picture beginning or ending with the given letters.

1. sn-

2. -ng

3. wh-

4. ch-

Listen and check the word.

1.
- [ ] whale
- [ ] thick
- [ ] bank

2.
- [ ] sing
- [ ] tank
- [ ] chick

3.
- [ ] flash
- [ ] swan
- [ ] snore

4.
- [ ] cheese
- [ ] shell
- [ ] bench

5.
- [ ] bath
- [ ] whisper
- [ ] teeth

6.
- [ ] stone
- [ ] sweet
- [ ] sink

Match and complete the word. Then write.

1.
sn •   • an   _____
sw •   • ail   _____

2.
pi •   • ng   _____
go •   • nk   _____

3.
ben •   • sh   _____
wa •   • ch   _____

4.
ch •   • air   _____
wh •   • isper   _____

5.
pi •   • sh   _____
di •   • nk   _____

6.
st •   • amp   _____
wh •   • ale   _____

● Match.

1.

ch- · ·

2.

wh- · ·

3.

-sh · ·

4.

gl- · ·

5.

-ng · ·

6.

dr- · ·

7.

-nk · ·

8.

tr- · ·

9.

bl- · ·

10.

sn- · ·

11.

sl- · ·

12.

th- · ·

Listen and circle the picture and the blending letters.

1. 　th-

　　-ng

2. 　tr-

　　sw-

3. 　br-

　　-ch

4. 　wh-

　　br-

5. 　pr-

　　-sh

6. 　ch-

　　bl-

7. 　sw-

　　-th

8. 　pr-

　　sm-

9. 　dr-

　　fr-

10. 　cr-

　　ch-

● Complete the word.

1.

__ __ a n e

2.
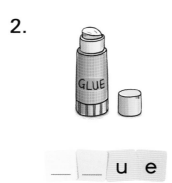
__ __ u e

3.

__ __ i d e

4.

__ __ o k e

5.

b a __ __

6.
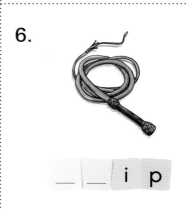
__ __ i p

7.
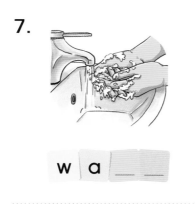
w a __ __

8.

b e n __ __

9.

__ __ i n t

10.

__ __ e l l

11.

__ __ i t e

12.

__ __ a n t

● Check the correct sentence for the picture.

1.
   - [ ] They are painting in art class.
   - [ ] They are playing the flute.

2.
   - [ ] A boy picked up gloves.
   - [ ] A boy picked up plums.

3.
   - [ ] A dragon is playing the trumpet.
   - [ ] A dragon is wearing a dress.

4.
   - [ ] A snail is swimming in the lake.
   - [ ] A snail is looking at the stones.

5.
   - [ ] They eat and drink at the table.
   - [ ] They sing and dance in the park.

6.
   - [ ] A boy is eating cheese.
   - [ ] A boy is looking at the shell.

Roll a die and move the number of the spaces. If you land on the picture, say the word for the picture and spell it. If the space has a sentence, follow the directions.

Start

Go over the bridge.

Say two words that end with NG.

Move back three steps.

Go over the bridge.

Go over the bridge.

Say two words that begin with WH.

STOP

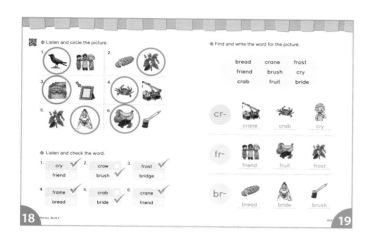

• Unit 3

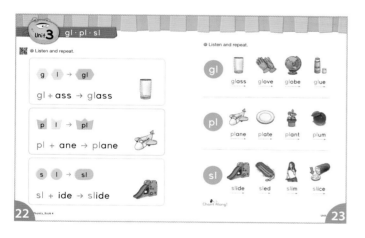

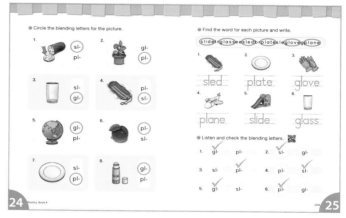

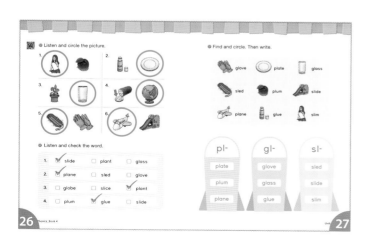

Student Book **Answers**

• Unit 4

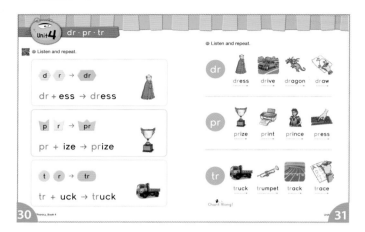

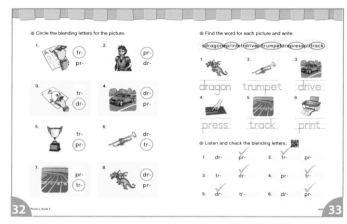

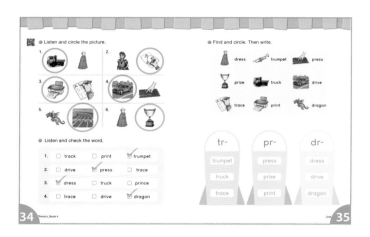

• Review 1

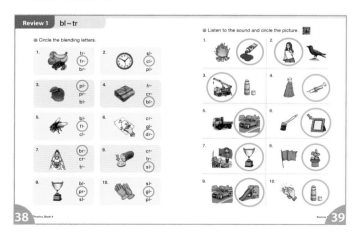

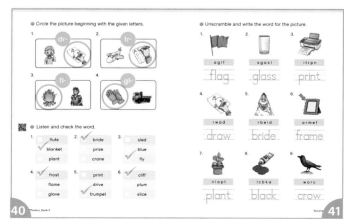

Unit 5

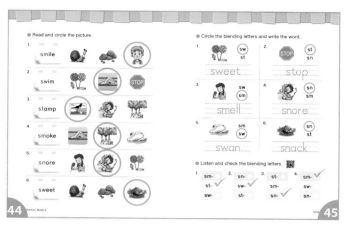

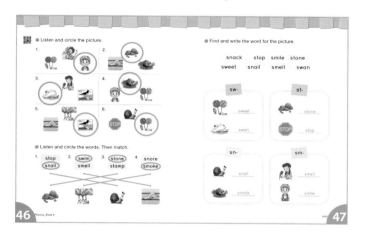

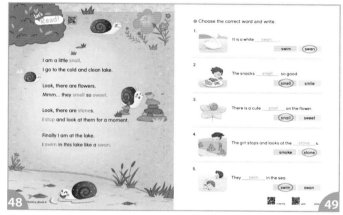

Unit 6

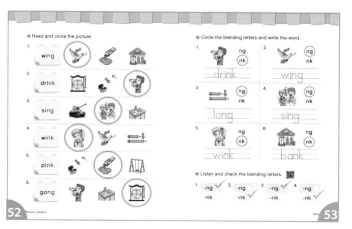

Student Book **Answers**

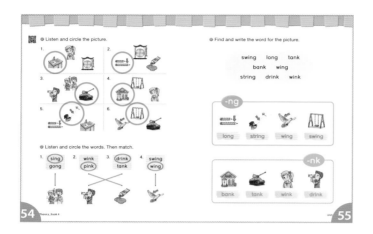

• Unit 7

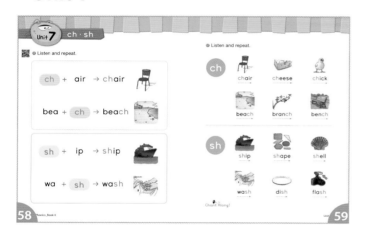

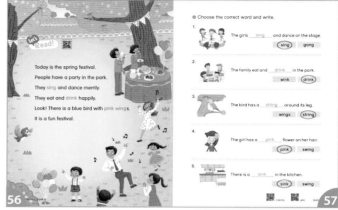

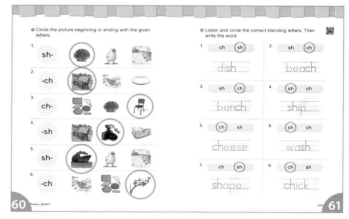

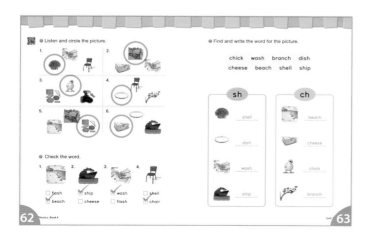

Unit 8

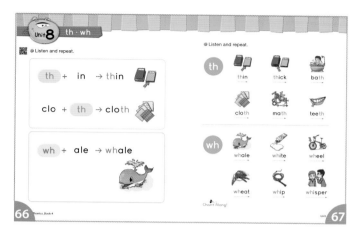

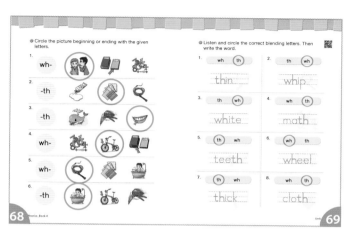

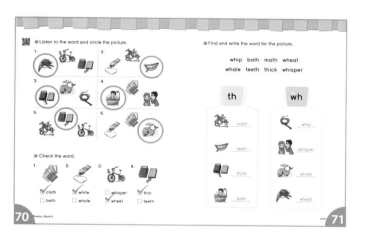

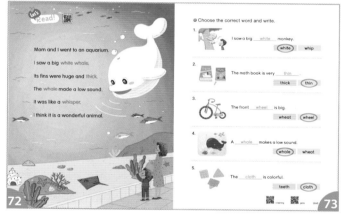

Review 2

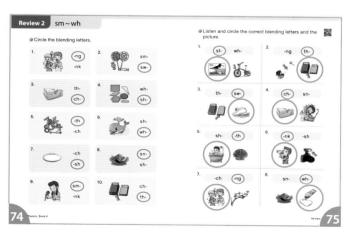

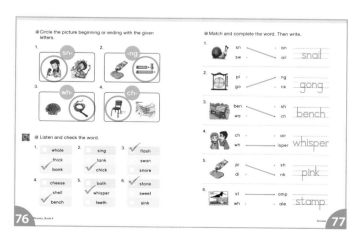

Student Book **Answers**

• Challenge

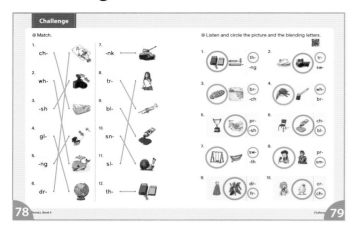

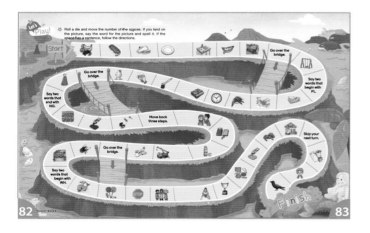

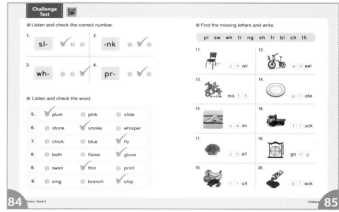

Workbook **Answers**

• Unit 1

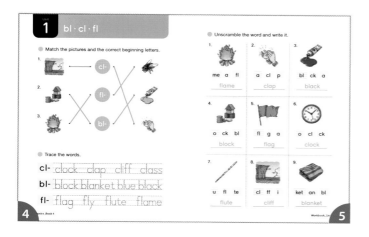

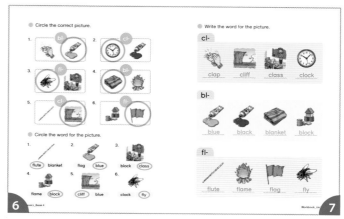

• Unit 2

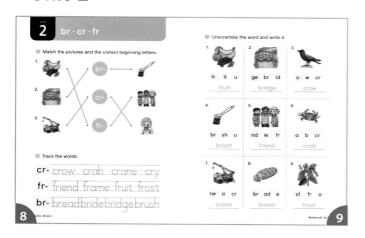

• Unit 3

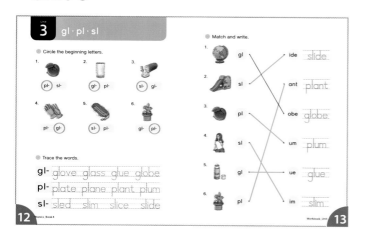

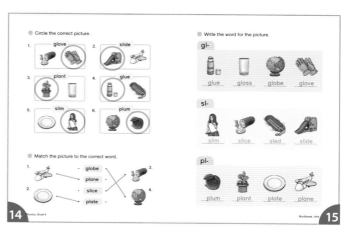

Workbook **Answers**

• Unit 4

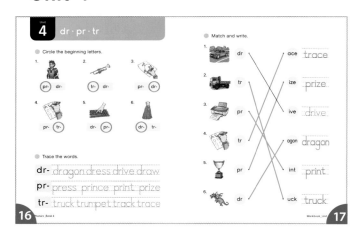

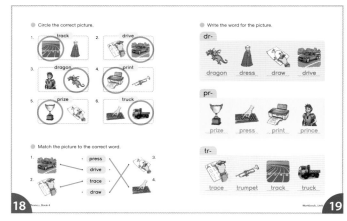

• Review 1

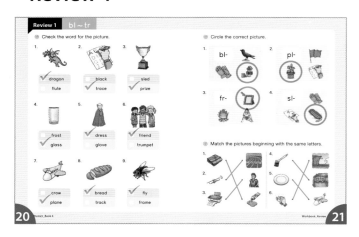

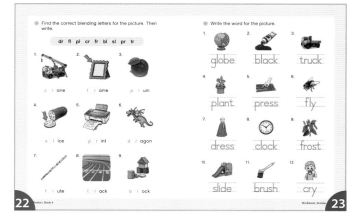

• Unit 5

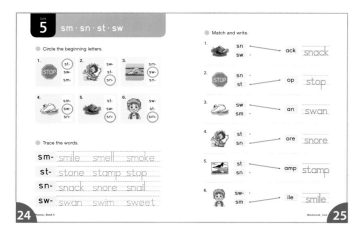

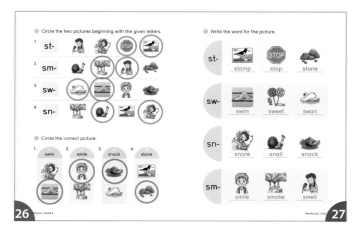

• Unit 6

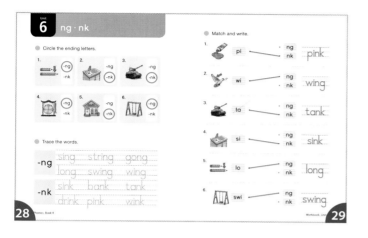

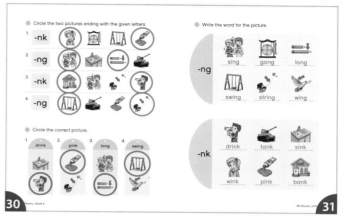

• Unit 7

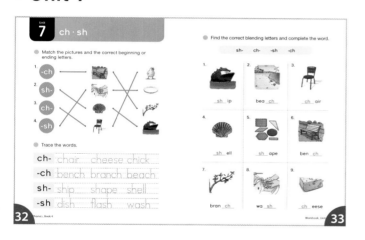

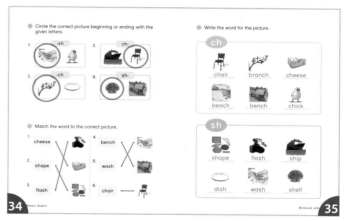

• Unit 8

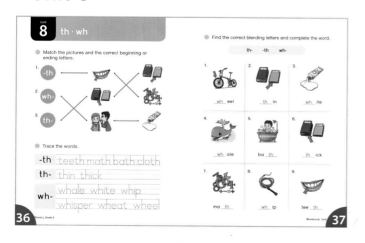

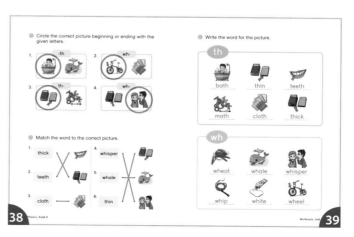

Workbook **Answers**

• Review 2

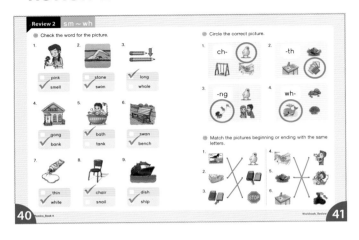

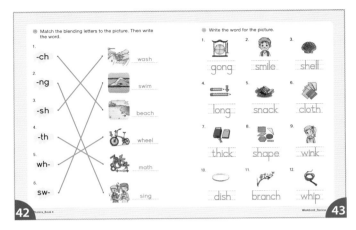

Final Test **Answers**

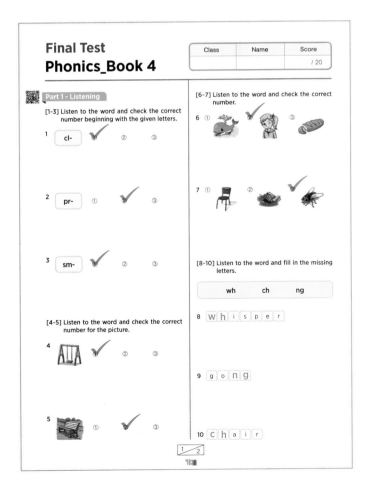

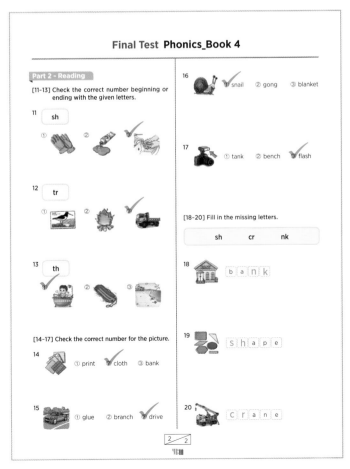

WORD CARDS

bl-

bl-

bl-

bl-

cl-

cl-

cl-

cl-

blue	blanket
block	black
class	clock
cliff	clap

WORD CARDS

fl-

fl-

fl-

fl-

br-

br-

br-

br-

fly	flag
flame	flute
bride	bread
brush	bridge

WORD CARDS

cr-

cr-

cr-

cr-

fr-

fr-

fr-

fr-

crab	crow
cry	crane
frame	friend
frost	fruit

WORD CARDS

gl-

gl-

gl-

gl-

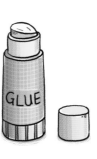

pl-

pl-

pl-

pl-

glove	glass
glue	globe
plate	plane
plum	plant

sl-

sl-

sl-

sl-

dr-

dr-

dr-

dr-

sled	slide
slice	slim
drive	dress
draw	dragon

WORD CARDS

pr-

pr-

pr-

pr-

tr-

tr-

tr-

tr-

print	prize
press	prince
trumpet	truck
trace	track

WORD CARDS

sm-

sm-

sm-

sn-

sn-

sn-

st-

st-

smell	smile
snail	smoke
snore	snack
stop	stamp

WORD CARDS

st-

sw-

sw-

sw-

-ng

-ng

-ng

-ng

swan	stone
sweet	swim
string	wing
swing	sing

WORD CARDS

-ng

-ng

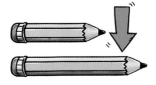

-nk

-nk

-nk

-nk

-nk

-nk

long	gong
sink	wink
drink	pink
tank	bank

WORD CARDS

ch-

ch-

ch-

-ch

-ch

-ch

sh-

sh-

cheese	chair
beach	chick
bench	branch
shape	ship

WORD CARDS

sh-

-sh

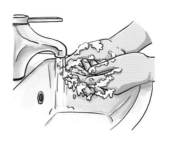

-sh

-sh

th-

th-

-th

-th

wash	shell
flash	dish
thick	thin
cloth	bath

WORD CARDS

-th

-th

wh-

wh-

wh-

wh-

wh-

wh-

teeth	math
white	whale
wheat	wheel
whisper	whip

BOOK
4

PHONICS
LAND

Double Letter Consonants

WORKBOOK

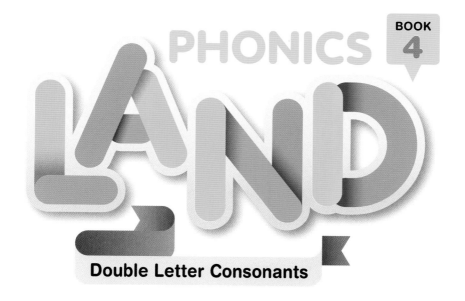

PHONICS

BOOK 4

LAND

Double Letter Consonants

WORKBOOK

YBM

Contents

⊙ Match the pictures and the correct beginning letters.

1.  •　•　cl- •　•　

2. •　•　fl- •　•　

3.  •　•　bl- •　•　

⊙ Trace the words.

| cl- | clock　clap　cliff　class |

| bl- | block blanket blue black |

| fl- | flag　fly　flute　flame |

Unscramble the word and write it.

1.

me	a	fl

_____

2.

a	cl	p

_____

3.

bl	ck	a

_____

4.

o	ck	bl

_____

5.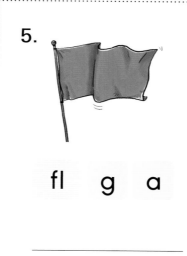

fl	g	a

_____

6.

o	cl	ck

_____

7.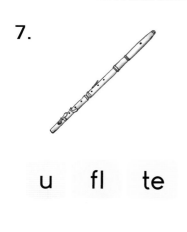

u	fl	te

_____

8.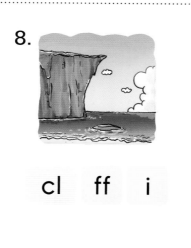

cl	ff	i

_____

9.

ket	an	bl

_____

Circle the correct picture.

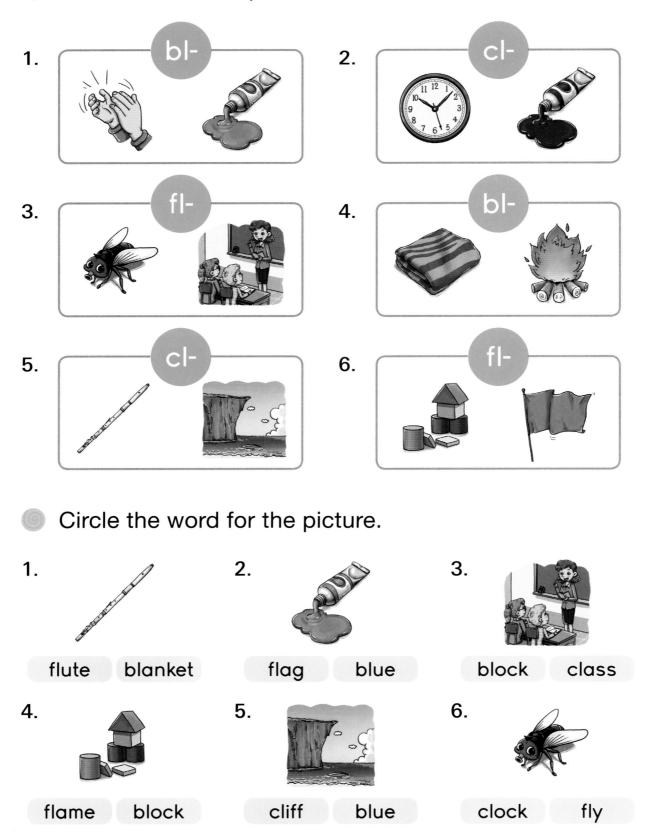

1. bl-
2. cl-
3. fl-
4. bl-
5. cl-
6. fl-

Circle the word for the picture.

1. flute   blanket
2. flag   blue
3. block   class
4. flame   block
5. cliff   blue
6. clock   fly

Write the word for the picture.

cl-

_____ _____ _____ _____

bl-

_____ _____ _____ _____

fl-

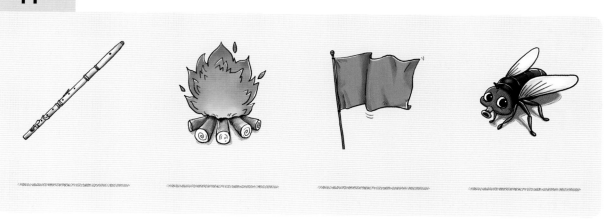

_____ _____ _____ _____

br · cr · fr

Match the pictures and the correct beginning letters.

1.  · ·  br- · ·

1.  · · (br-)· ·

2.  · · (cr-)· ·

3.  · · (fr-)· ·

Trace the words.

cr- crow crab crane cry

fr- friend frame fruit frost

br- bread bride bridge brush

Unscramble the word and write it.

1.

fr　it　u

_____

2.
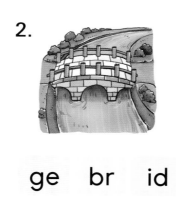

ge　br　id

_____

3.

o　w　cr

_____

4.

br　sh　u

_____

5.

nd　ie　fr

_____

6.

a　b　cr

_____

7.
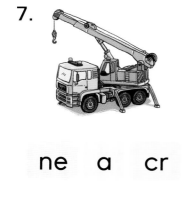

ne　a　cr

_____

8.
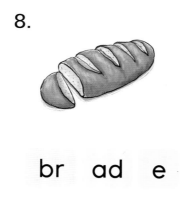

br　ad　e

_____

9.

st　fr　o

_____

Circle the correct picture.

1. cr-

2. br-

3. cr-

4. fr-

5. fr-

6. br-

Circle the word for the picture.

1. crane   brush

2. crow   bridge

3. bread   frame

4. friend   crane

5. brush   friend

6. bride   crab

Write the word for the picture.

br-

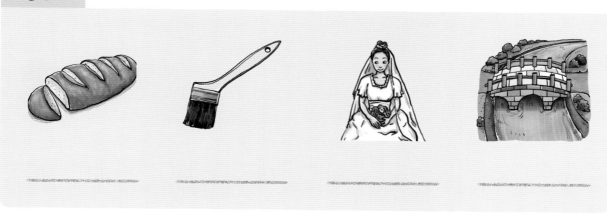

cr-

fr-

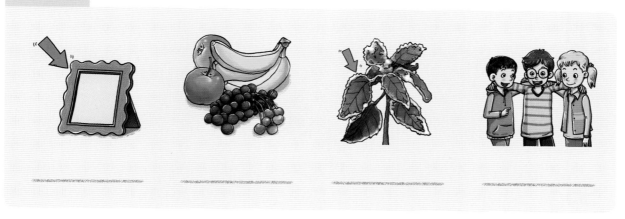

Circle the beginning letters.

1.

pl-   sl-

2.

gl-   pl-

3.

sl-   gl-

4.

pl-   gl-

5.

sl-   pl-

6.

gl-   pl-

Trace the words.

gl-   glove glass glue globe

pl-   plate plane plant plum

sl-   sled   slim   slice slide

Match and write.

1.  gl • | • ide _____

2. 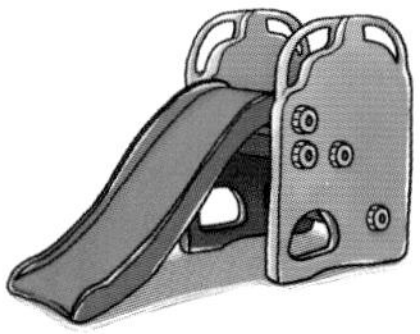 sl • | • ant _____

3.  pl • | • obe globe

4.  sl • | • um _____

5. 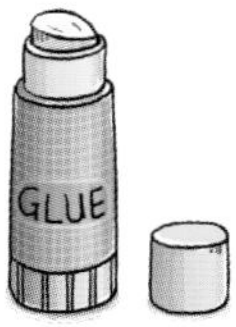 gl • | • ue _____

6.  pl • | • im _____

Ⓒ Circle the correct picture.

1. glove

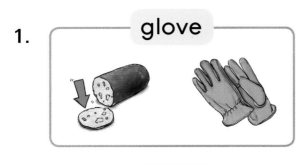

2. slide

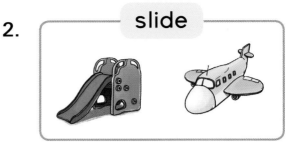

3. plant

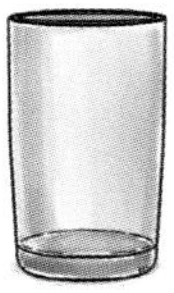

4. glue

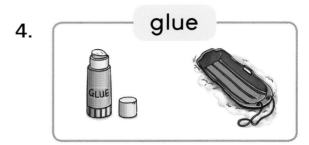

5. slim

6. plum

Ⓒ Match the picture to the correct word.

1.

2.

• globe •

• plane •

• slice •

• plate •

3.

4.

Write the word for the picture.

gl-

_____ _____ _____ _____

sl-

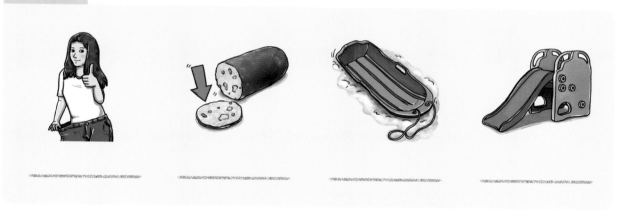

_____ _____ _____ _____

pl-

_____ _____ _____ _____

○ Circle the beginning letters.

1.

pr-   dr-

2.

tr-   dr-

3.

pr-   dr-

4.

pr-   tr-

5.

dr-   pr-

6.

dr-   tr-

○ Trace the words.

dr- dragon dress drive draw

pr- press prince print prize

tr- truck trumpet track trace

Match and write.

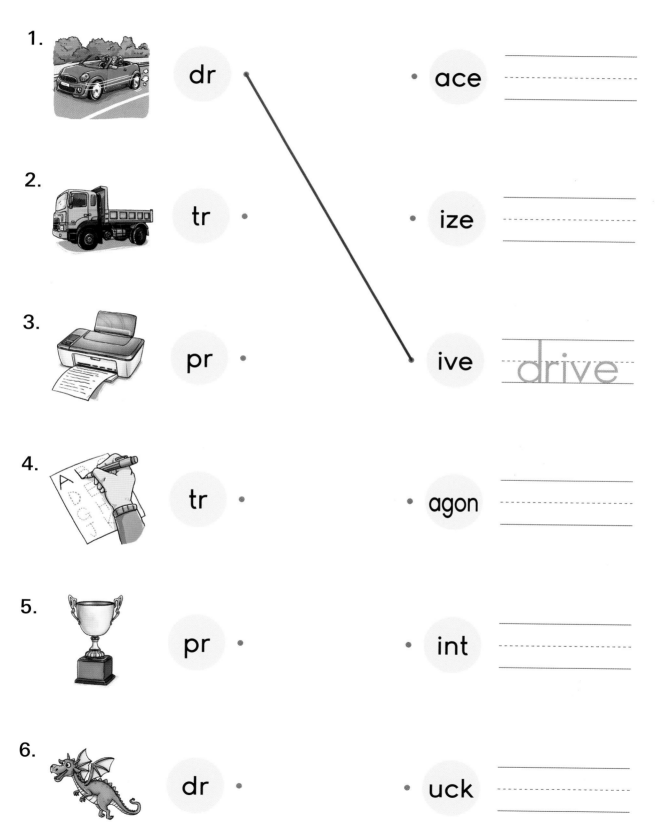

1. dr • • ace _____

2. tr • • ize _____

3. pr • • ive drive

4. tr • • agon _____

5. pr • • int _____

6. dr • • uck _____

Circle the correct picture.

1. **track**

2. **drive**

3. **dragon**

4. **print**

5. **prize**

6. **truck**

Match the picture to the correct word.

1.

3.

• press •

• drive •

2.

• trace •

4.

• draw •

Write the word for the picture.

dr-

pr-

tr-

Check the word for the picture.

1.

☐ dragon

☐ flute

2.

☐ black

☐ trace

3.

☐ sled

☐ prize

4.

☐ frost

☐ glass

5.

☐ dress

☐ glove

6.

☐ friend

☐ trumpet

7.

☐ crow

☐ plane

8.

☐ bread

☐ track

9.

☐ fly

☐ frame

🌀 Circle the correct picture.

1.
bl-

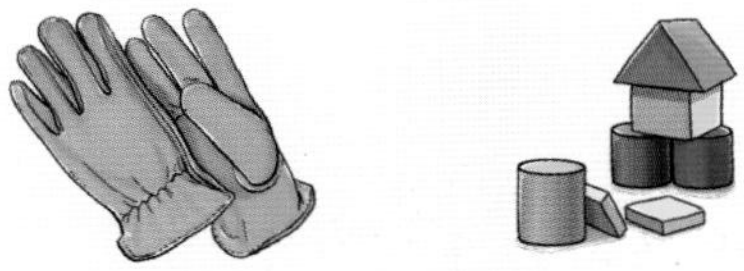

2.
pl-

3.
fr-

4.
sl-

🌀 Match the pictures beginning with the same letters.

1.

•
•

4.

•
•

2.

•
•

5.

•
•

3.

•
•

6.
•
•

Find the correct blending letters for the picture. Then write.

dr fl pl cr fr bl sl pr tr

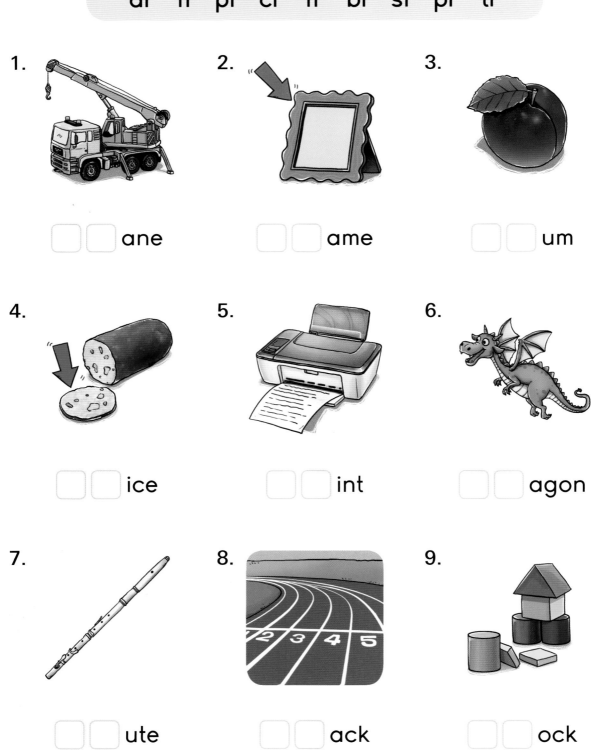

1. ☐☐ ane

2. ☐☐ ame

3. ☐☐ um

4. ☐☐ ice

5. ☐☐ int

6. ☐☐ agon

7. ☐☐ ute

8. ☐☐ ack

9. ☐☐ ock

@ Write the word for the picture.

1.

2.

3.

4.

5.

6.

7.

8.

9.

10.

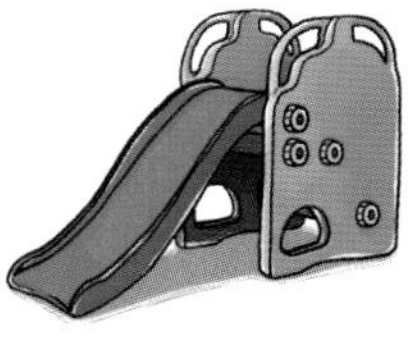

11.

12.

Circle the beginning letters.

1.
st-
sw-
sm-

2.
sw-
st-
sn-

3.
sm-
sw-
sn-

4.
sm-
sw-
sn-

5.
st-
sw-
sn-

6.
sw-
st-
sm-

Trace the words.

sm-	smile smell smoke
st-	stone stamp stop
sn-	snack snore snail
sw-	swan swim sweet

Match and write.

1. 
sn •
sw •

• ack _____

2. 
sn •
st •

• op _____

3. 
sw •
sm •

• an _____

4. 
st •
sn •

• ore _____

5. 
st •
sn •

• amp _____

6. 
sw- •
sm •

• ile _____

Circle the two pictures beginning with the given letters.

1. st-

2. sm-

3. sw-

4. sn-

Circle the correct picture.

1. swim

2. smile

3. snack

4. stone

Write the word for the picture.

st-

sw-

sn-

sm-

Circle the ending letters.

1.
-ng
-nk

2.
-ng
-nk

3.
-ng
-nk

4.
-ng
-nk

5.
-ng
-nk

6.
-ng
-nk

Trace the words.

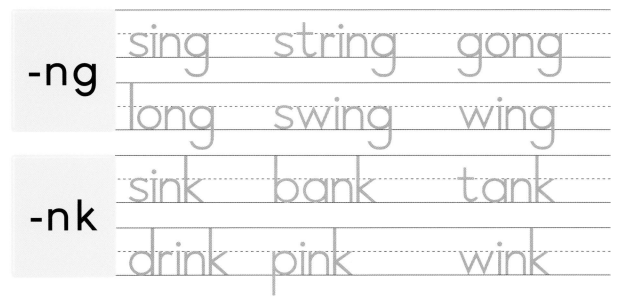

-ng
sing string gong
long swing wing

-nk
sink bank tank
drink pink wink

Match and write.

1. pi •
   • ng ———————
   • nk ———————

2. wi •
   • ng ———————
   • nk ———————

3. ta •
   • ng ———————
   • nk ———————

4. si •
   • ng ———————
   • nk ———————

5. lo •
   • ng ———————
   • nk ———————

6. swi •
   • ng ———————
   • nk ———————

Circle the two pictures ending with the given letters.

1. **-nk**

2. **-ng**

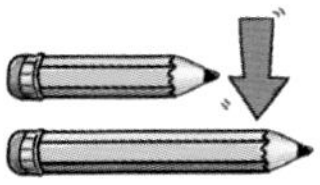

3. **-nk**

4. **-ng**

Circle the correct picture.

1. drink

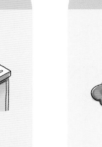

2. pink

3. long

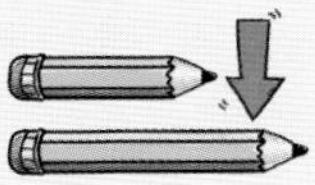

4. swing

Write the word for the picture.

-ng

-nk

Match the pictures and the correct beginning or ending letters.

1. **-ch** · · 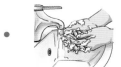 · ·

2. **sh-** · ·  · ·

3. **ch-** · ·  · ·

4. **-sh** · ·

Trace the words.

ch-	chair cheese chick
-ch	bench branch beach
sh-	ship shape shell
-sh	dish flash wash

Find the correct blending letters and complete the word.

sh-   ch-   -sh   -ch

1.

_____ ip

2.

bea _____

3.

_____ air

4.

_____ ell

5.

_____ ape

6.

ben _____

7.

bran _____

8.

wa _____

9.

_____ eese

Circle the correct picture beginning or ending with the given letters.

1. **-sh**

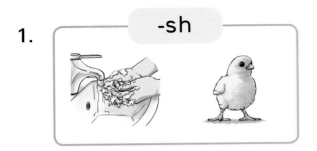

2. **ch-**

3. **-ch**

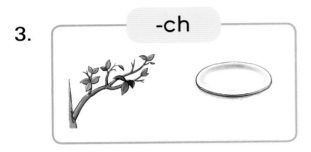

4. **sh-**

Match the word to the correct picture.

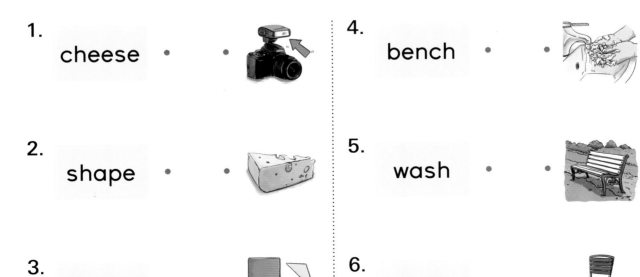

1. cheese •

2. shape •

3. flash •

4. bench •

5. wash •

6. chair •

Write the word for the picture.

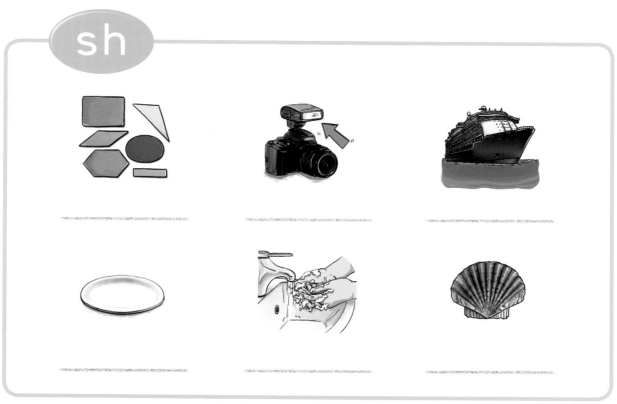

Match the pictures and the correct beginning or ending letters.

1.   •   •

2.   •   •

3.   •   •

Trace the words.

-th	teeth math bath cloth
th-	thin thick
wh-	whale white whip
	whisper wheat wheel

Find the correct blending letters and complete the word.

th-   -th   wh-

1.

_____ eel

2.

_____ in

3.

_____ ite

4.

_____ ale

5.

ba _____

6.

_____ ick

7.

ma _____

8.

_____ ip

9.

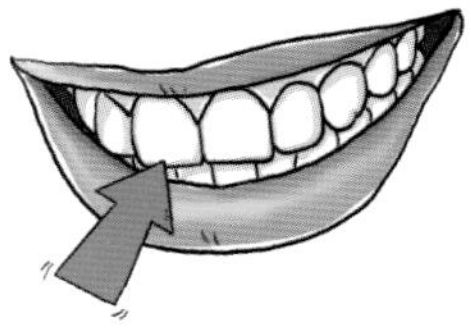

tee _____

Circle the correct picture beginning or ending with the given letters.

1. **-th**

2. **wh-**

3. **th-**

4. **wh-**

Match the word to the correct picture.

1. thick •

•

2. teeth •

•

3. cloth •

•

4. whisper •

•

5. whale •

•

6. thin •

•

Write the word for the picture.

🌀 Check the word for the picture.

1.

- [ ] pink
- [ ] smell

2.

- [ ] stone
- [ ] swim

3.

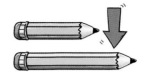

- [ ] long
- [ ] whale

4.

- [ ] gong
- [ ] bank

5.

- [ ] bath
- [ ] tank

6.

- [ ] swan
- [ ] bench

7.

- [ ] thin
- [ ] white

8.

- [ ] chair
- [ ] snail

9.

- [ ] dish
- [ ] ship

Circle the correct picture.

1. ch-

2. -th

3. -ng

4. wh-

Match the pictures beginning or ending with the same letters.

1.  • •

2.  • •

3.  • •

4. 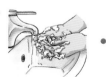 • •

5.  • •

6.  • •

🌀 Match the blending letters to the picture. Then write the word.

1.

-ch •

• _____

2.

-ng •

• _____

3.

-sh •

• _____

4.

-th •

• _____

5.

wh- •

• _____

6.

sw- •

• _____

@ Write the word for the picture.

1.

2.

3.

4.

5.

6.

7.

8.

9.

10.

11.

12.

Memo